To J

KEEPING YOUR
COMMITMENT

ISBN: 1-4196-8013-7

ISBN-13: 9781419680137

Visit www.booksurge.com to order additional copies.

KEEPING YOUR COMMITMENT

Plain Advice for Engaged
and
Newlywed Couples

(Workbook included)

Risa Pleasant

Dedicated to the Moms

Ruth and Jacqueline
for
Rhonda, Rhea, and *John Gregory*

Acknowledgements

My husband Mark (for 27 years of marriage)
Candis (for your friendship)

Table of Contents

Introduction

We have spent the last sixteen years ministering in the areas of marriage and family. In no way are we experts in these fields, but we have lots of life experience. After years of teaching, lecturing, and peer mentoring, we have witnessed a pattern of rectifiable mistakes most newly weds make that wreck their marriages. It is our hope that this book will help newly wed couples avoid these same mistakes.

Most couples learn what little they know about marriage from the life experiences of those around them—mom and dad, siblings, other family, and friends.

What we think is wonderful about the Christian marriage is that there is always a present help in the time of crisis. That help is of course our Savior, Jesus Christ.

We have discovered in our own relationship that following His blueprint for marriage and life always works. Therefore, we would like to share some of the mistakes we have made and seen others make and hopefully pass on a way to avoid them in your marriage. We pray they will bless your marriage as they certainly have blessed ours.

Sincerely,
Mark & Risa Pleasant

What about Divorce?

This list details how we react to the divorce or separation of someone we love and respect.

1. We are frightened and we fear that it may somehow happen to us, as though it was something we could catch.

2. We are suddenly aware of the shortcomings of our own marriage.

3. We are filled with tremendous doubt. It is a real life tragedy happening to people just like us. After all, if they are just like us, can't this happen in our relationship?

4. No marriage ever reaches a point where it is immune to failure. We think our marriage is different but we must continue to work at marriage with the same excellence we commit to other projects that are important.

5. We allow a host of uncertainties and worries to creep into our own relationship. We can become deeply entangled in the details of a divorce by silently comparing the divorced marriage to our own. For example, if a friend attributes her divorce to her husband spending too much time at the office, we begin thinking maybe my husband is too involved in his career.

6. We may become suspicious or anxious if a friend's spouse is involved in an affair. These comparisons can lead to bickering, arguments, and feelings of ill will that make our relationship

all the more vulnerable. Learn to talk these feelings out with your spouse.

7. We do not want to address or confront the issues that surface. Nobody likes confrontation because it makes us uncomfortable. However, it is easier to save a marriage that is having some trouble than try to resurrect one that is over. Out of confrontation comes growth and out of growth comes maturity.

8. All marriages have problems. It is safe to assume that other marriages are not that much different from our own. The only difference between us and another couple is they may have thrown in the towel and we may have chosen to stay in the ring.

Can You Divorce-proof Your Marriage?
(You can certainly try)

Here is how:

- Pray, pray, pray for your marriage and your spouse

- On a daily basis, study the Word or have devotions together

- Take note of sudden changes in the atmosphere of your marriage like boredom, spending less time together, avoidance, etc.

- Spend time talking with each other to catch up on what the other is thinking or going through

- Ten minutes a day talking about what's on your mind can make a big difference

- Periodically ask each other, "Are we OK? Too distant? Out of touch with each other's lives? Do we have enough intimate time together?"

- Continue to date. The anticipation keeps the romance fresh and alive!

- Avoid spending time with people who have bad marriages, or who are disrespectful to the needs of their spouse. How can two walk together unless they agree? One of the worst things for a marriage is being friends with a couple who has a warped or jacked up perspective on marriage.

• Grow up! Children are the only people who constantly want their own way. The real destroyer of marriage is selfishness, putting our wants and needs ahead of our family unit. We can tear our own marriage and family apart. We ruin the lives of others by our own self-centeredness. Phrases like "I need my own space, I need more time for myself, and I feel stifled by the marriage" are sure signs your marriage is in serious trouble. Don't wait, get help!

• Don't spend a great deal of time with someone of the opposite sex that is not your mate, even if it's ministry time like prayer. Whomever we spend the most time with is who we will bond with.

• To whom much is given, much is required. We cannot have prominence, position, and people's respect and not work on our home life. It comes with the territory. When we fall publicly we hurt more than just our immediate family. We leave a big gaping wound in the Body of Christ. Think about recent well-known pastors and evangelists who have fallen, divorced their spouses, committed adultery, and all kinds of sexual sin. How did it make you feel? It makes us all hurt. Now, think about the people who love and respect you, did you know that they secretly want you to have a successful marriage? It gives them hope that they too can make it! Did you know if our divorce or separation causes another to backslide, God will hold it to our account?

• Today I am much more impressed when I meet someone who has been married over thirty years than I am with the CEO of a major corporation, because marriage is harder work!

Commitment is the Key

Mistake # 1: It's not about love!

In actuality, it is not love, but commitment, honoring the vow that we made that keeps good marriages together. They are some days we just don't feel so in love with your spouse because they have upset or disappointed us. That's called life, get over it and move forward.

An old song by Tina Turner says, *"What's love got to do with it?"* When it comes to long term marriages, love definitely isn't everything. Believe it or not, it is not love that makes couples stick it out during tough or hard times. It is commitment! People fall in and out of love everyday. I have actually seen couples who say they are hopelessly in love only to find out three months later they cannot stand to be in the same room together. Love obviously didn't keep them together. I once attended the wedding of a couple and was looking forward to seeing them on Sunday following the honeymoon. I'd heard they were back in town, but what I saw as they entered the church stunned me. The loving couple only a week earlier was now sitting on opposite sides of the sanctuary. They obviously had love but no commitment.

Today you are going to need a lot more than love to make it past the following US census bureau statistics:

- The median duration of today's marriage is less than seven years.

- 50% of marriages will end in divorce, including Christian marriages.

- 60% of remarriages will end in divorce.

- Second marriages on average end four years earlier than the first marriage.

- The average number of Americans divorcing each year is approximately 2.5 million.

- 3.8 million people prefer living together rather than getting married.

- *Fatherless homes account for 63% of youth suicides, 90% of homeless/runaway children, 85% of children with behavior problems, 71% of high school drop outs, 85% of youth in prison, and well over 50% of teen mothers. *(Divorce Magazine & American for Divorce Reform)

- The state with the lowest divorce rate is Massachusetts (2 for every 1,000 people)

- The state with the highest divorce rate is Nevada (9 for every 1,000 people)

- Virginia is ranked 25th surprisingly behind California which ranked 21st

- Children of divorced parents are 50% more likely to divorce after they marry

- 80% of divorces filed are for irreconcilable differences.

How is it possible these same couples who were madly in love at one time end up in court with differences so insurmountable that they are irreconcilable? Some very common mistakes and unrealistic expectations may be the cause.

We have heard it said over and over again that we live in a disposable society. We throw away what we don't want and get a new one. It is the same with marriages and children. We simply toss out the old family and get a newer model. We have witnessed a disturbing trend lately. People leave their spouses and have nothing to do with their children because they aren't cut out for parenting. These people later remarry and have more children. What was wrong with the original spouse and first set of children? We've ended up with a generation of people who are committed to nothing but themselves and short-term self-gratification.

This is a generation that spends their time doing what pleases them and finds no pleasure in caring or sharing life's joys with another. We all know people who spend boundless energy and time being the best at their jobs while allowing their marriages to fall apart.

Being married isn't easy and it takes a lot of compromise to be successful at it. But it is a tremendous reward when it works. Marriage is literally a reflection of God's love and passion for the Church. His creation, Adam, was incredible and perfect, and once God created Eve; Adam had a partner and was no longer alone. Marriage takes as much commitment and dedication as a job. On the job, we can be replaced, but no one can replace the role God specifically designed for you in your own family unit.

Lack of commitment in marriage has left us with a messed up generation of children. They have grown up on TV, movies, computers, and video games. I hold onto the hope that they will one day do great things for Christ. We must remember we created them, yet instead of giving them our time and attention, we give them money, luxury items, and the task to fend for themselves.

If our children have witnessed commitment, even in the most difficult of times, they learn compromise, negotiation, and the will to see things through to the end. We have raised a generation that doesn't have the fortitude to read a book, so how can we expect them to be committed to marriage? We must honor our commitment to marriage. Learning to honor a promise at an early age is an important step to staying married. Marriage is commitment. Keep your commitment, your vow, and your promise!

Old Things are
Passed Away, Right?

Mistake # 2: Underestimating Generational Curses

If you are not careful you can find yourself reliving your parents' bad marriage.

Generational curses play a major role in some very common mistakes made by newly married couples. Did you ever say, "When I grow up, I'm never going to be like my parents"? Many of us find years later that we are exactly like our parents. When I was a girl, my mother had an annoying habit of digging in her purse while driving. It drove my sisters and me crazy! We'd yell "Mom, what are you looking for? Keep your eyes on the road!" That habit bugged us so much so that we swore to never repeat it. Years later my daughter is irritated because, you guessed it, I dig through my purse while driving, and so does my younger sister! When I say or do something that my parents would have said or done, I find myself saying, "Whoa! Where did that come from"?

Children who grew up in a home where their parents yelled and screamed all the time, begin to see this as normal behavior, so it's very possible to repeat this same behavior in a marriage. For the child who grows up in quiet household, being married to someone with this aggressive pattern of behavior can be a nightmare. The child who watches their father cheat on their mother while the mother turns a blind eye may also assume this is acceptable behavior and find themselves attracted to someone with the same personality trait. The same goes for the child growing up in a home of sexual abuse, violence, alcoholism, poverty, illegitimacy, and drug abuse. These are all examples of generational curses that can run in families and are quite often passed on from one generation to the next. Depression, emotional problems and mental health issues can also be a part of a family's history. Remember to recognize what issues your particular family struggles with and pray about breaking these curses over your family. Do whatever needs to be done to break these chains; seek professional help through medical, psychological, psychiatric, pastoral, or Theophostic treatment.

The sins of the father go to the third and fourth generation, but the blessings of God goes to thousand generations. Deuteronomy 5:9-10

Wouldn't you rather reject those old family curses and chains? Rebuke those family behaviors and life patterns, covenant with God to walk in blessing. If we do not acknowledge and denounce these behaviors and life patterns through a relationship with Jesus Christ, we find our selves hopelessly repeating the same mistakes over and over again. Praise God there is a way out, spend some alone time with God ask Him to show you areas of your family history that could potentially destroy your marriage. Knowledge is power.

My people perish for the lack of knowledge. Hosea 4:6

Write down these hindrances and commit to pray daily against them. Remind yourself you are a new creation in Christ. There is a ton of help out there, so get a hold of it. Just because your dad beat your mom up doesn't mean you have to repeat it. Ask God to close the door that allowed this to control your family.

Therefore if any man be in Christ, he is a new creature; old things are passed away behold, all things are become new. 2 Corinthians 5:17

Compensation for My Pain and Suffering!

Mistake # 3: Hold onto the past

Failure to let go of the past may just destroy the future of your new marriage.

In this world of addictive and abusive behavior, many of us walk with lots of emotional baggage. Some people stay stuck in the muck of a traumatic childhood and bring that emotional baggage into marriage. The average person doesn't seek treatment that is so easily accessible today, but Christian counselors and therapists are out there and open for business. The intimacies of marriage pop open the locks on all that baggage. Once the suitcase is open, it's difficult but not impossible to close it again. Many unsuspecting spouses find themselves paying the price for the pain and suffering inflicted on their spouse at the hands of another. Marriage is difficult enough to navigate without bringing a load of emotional baggage. Why should your spouse be the one to compensate you for you pain? If these unresolved conflicts from the past resurface and are allowed to fester, couples will shut down emotionally and be unable to enjoy the blessing God intended for their marriage.

I cannot urge you enough to seek professional counseling before taking marriage vows. Some traumatic experiences need more than just an altar call, although some people have been instantly healed during a service. Many others need help to walk it out. Mark and I strongly believe in counseling prior to taking the leap into marriage and strongly recommend taking Marriage and Family classes the first two years of marriage. Both greatly increases your chances of staying married.

Stand fast in the liberty wherewith Christ hath made us free, and be not entangled again with the yoke of bondage. Galatians 5:1

Get free, stay free!

No Hitting Below the Belt (Fight Fair)

Mistake # 4: Fighting Ugly

When it comes to arguing, you can win the battle, but lose the war. Too many couples use the "no-holds-barred" method of arguing, which is a recipe for disaster.

Confrontation is a normal part of married life; however, there should be common rules of engagement before fighting, which will make life simpler. Why do we hurt the one we love the most? The following are some tips on "fair fighting" to help you not go below the belt!

- Don't start name-calling—this is your marriage not the schoolyard. Mark and I are blown away by the names couples call each other and low they can sink during an argument. Having an argument is a normal part of married life; however, going for the juggler is not normal.

- Never, ever use ethnic or racial slurs against each other. We have actually seen interracial couples get divorced because they went down that road. One interracial couple we knew started arguing and began name-calling and went too far, because winning the argument was more important to them than exercising self-control. We've told our former students you can win the battle and lose the war. I talked to couples who have done this very thing and are divorced because they went so far out there they passed the point of no return. You can so offend your spouse with words so painful they may never be able to get over it. We've seen it happen.

- Never bring family members or friends into an argument or tell them things about your argument. After the fight, you may forgive your spouse, but your family or friends may not be so gracious.

- Don't bring up old stuff, but stay in the moment. Get it straight right then and it won't have to be revisited.

- There is never an excuse to get physical! Couples, especially Christians, should never invade the others personal space, grab, shake, or strike their mate when trying to make a point. Take a break, cool down, and pick up the matter later when cooler heads prevail.

- Allow your spouse to express an opinion while arguing. Don't interrupt. Validate their feelings no matter how absurd their point may be to you. The very fact that they're expressing it has merit.

- Most couples don't hear each other while arguing because each one is so busy defending their own position and thinking of their great "comeback" line or "fight-winning" comment.

When Mark and I peer-counsel (mentor) with a couple, one of the most important things we do is allow each spouse to express their opinion, without interruption by their spouse. We ask the spouse if they understood and sometimes ask them to repeat what the other said. In many situations this alone acts as a catalyst and we almost never have to see these couples again. They realize that sometimes you just need to listen.

Let every man be quick to listen, but slow to use his tongue, and slow to loose his temper.
James 1:19-20

Things to Remember

- Ask God's direction and timing when trying to discuss difficult issues

- Don't start an argument with accusatory statements like *"you always" or "you never".*

- Remember your spouse is not the enemy, the other team, or the target! You're on the same team, same playing field, and in the same game.

- Keep family out of your business and set rules and boundaries when it comes to them.

- Husbands, defend your wife to your family, no matter what, *especially if you plan on staying married to her!*

- Wives, let the responsibility of the family fall back on the husband. Let him suffer the consequences if things don't work and try not to fix it for him. Remember, he is the head of the family.

- Taking marriage, parenting, or family classes the first two years of marriage actually significantly improves your chances of staying married.

- Make yourself accountable to a pastor or spiritual leader if you are having problems.

- Get into a small group with other married couples.

- Try to find a marriage mentor in the form of another happily married couple.

- Get counseling for extreme or unresolved emotional problems.

*Please note if you are in a dangerous situation such as mental and/ or physical abuse, please report it to the police or someone who can help you. God's Biblical plan for marriage does not include physical, verbal, or emotional abuse!

A soft answer turns away wrath, but a harsh word stirs up anger. Proverb 15:1

Forgiveness

Mistake # 5: being unyielding and unforgiving

Failure to forgive can guarantee a rough and rocky marriage

Have you ever met someone who is bitter? They are angry with everyone, get made about nothing, and are extremely critical and difficult to get along with. The root cause of bitterness is unforgiveness. Forgiveness is a given when it comes to marriage. Unforgiveness is one of the reasons, if not the biggest, that our prayers go unanswered. If you refuse to forgive, God can't forgive you. If He can't forgive you, then He certainly can't answer your prayers. We live in a world where stuff happens. Is life sometimes unfair, injustice, and cruel? Yes, but hanging onto the past will keep us from enjoying the future.

I once new someone whose bitterness and life disappointments consumed him until he was a depressed, lonely, critical old man who died without any family love or close friendships. He hadn't been particularly kind to me, but I remember breaking down and crying at his funeral, because something in me broke. I loved him in spite of it; and had so much to tell him, share with him, talk to him about, learn about him. Unfortunately his bitterness kept me more than arms distance away.

Don't let unhappy memories consume you. Don't let your loved ones suffer because you were hurt by others. Seek professional help.

Freely forgive, as the Lord has forgiven you. Colossians 3:13

Remember to:

- Forgive immediately and daily
- Ask God to help you not to pick up offenses against your spouse or others.
- True forgiveness means you don't want revenge.
- Forgiveness heals and sets us free from hurt. It does not absolve the one who has done us harm, it simply frees us up to be open to God's forgiveness and people's love.
- Some things seem unforgivable, but still require it from God. Sexual abuse and physical battery have destroyed and crushed the spirits of many. Although you must forgive, these are crimes and are punishable under the laws of the land. If the one you love is committing these atrocities, please report it to the authorities!
- Communicate and compromise. Only children expect to always get their way. Someone has to be the grownup in the relationship, why not let it be you?
- Love doesn't keep record of wrong doing.
- If you stay married long enough, your spouse will disappoint you or hurt your feelings and you will do the same to them. Forgive, get over it, and move on toward the marriage God intended for you.

Be ready to forgive others as God, for Christ's sake has forgiven you. Ephesians 4:32

My Work Here is Finished!

Mistake # 6: Letting the romance die

Keep passion alive by stoking the fires of love.

Many couples feel that dating ends the moment marriage begins. Dating should remain an integral part of marriage, especially after you have children. The best thing children can have is two parents who love each other. It makes them feel so secure and safe. Remember, to keep a fire going you have to stir the embers, fan the flames, and add more fuel to the fire!

It is obvious that the mind can be forgetful or the Lord would not have admonished us to renew it by reading His Word daily. Dating helps us to renew passion, spark excitement, and remind us of why we chose to marry this person in the first place. If you make dating a regular part of your routine from the beginning, it will help you keep your focus on each other even after having children. Moms really need this because they spend the majority of their time with the children, so she needs adult conversation, to be touched, and positive verbal reinforcement from her husband.

Couples who divorce during the "empty nest" years (after the kids have left home) have a common complaint. They spent the marriage focusing on the kids and not each other; therefore, they no longer know each other or care deeply enough to stay in the marriage. To avoid this, keep dating and focused on each other as well as the children.

Tips on dating your spouse:

• Plan dates and put them on the calendar.

• Husbands, don't expect the wife to do it all!

• Keep a reliable and trustworthy babysitter available.

• Date at least once a month, ideally weekly.

• If you rent videos for your date, skip the porn and horror.

• Put your kids to bed. By the way, all children should have a set bedtime every night. Children need order and discipline, because it makes them feel secure and the household is less chaotic.

• Don't talk about bills and how you are going to pay them.

• Focus on talking to each and not about the kids.

• Don't bring up past arguments or try to resolve issues. This is about romance.

Dates don't always have to cost a lot of money or any money at all! The following are great inexpensive date ideas:

• Picnic on the floor after the kids are asleep

• Watch the sunset together at a romantic spot

• Take a site-seeing drive together

• Walk along the beach

• Tour a local nature park, zoo, or botanical garden

• Go bike riding

- Roller skate

- Have a candle-light dinner at home and dress up a little

- Sit on the same side at a restaurant and share dessert

- Go to a matinee or twilight movie (less expensive) and share a bucket of popcorn and a drink

- Get an ice cream cone, sit outside, and talk

- Throw loose change in a jar to save money for dates

Live happily with the woman you love through the fleeting days of life, for the wife God gives you is your best reward down here for all your earthly toil. Ecclesiastes 9:9

Sex is Important!

Mistake # 7: Letting Go of Intimacy

S ex is important. If you're not having it, you're just roommates and not spouses!

The man should give his all and the wife should do the same for her husband. For a girl who marries no longer has full right to her to her own body, for her husband then has his rights to it, too; and in the same way the husband no longer has full right to his own body, for it belongs also to his wife. So do not refuse these rights to each other. The only exception to rule would be the agreement of both husband and wife to refrain from the rights of marriage for a limited time, so that they can give themselves more completely to prayer. Afterwards, they should come together again so that Satan won't be able to tempt them because of their lack of self – control. 1 Corinthians 7:3-5

Sex has become so perverted in this world that nobody with any decency wants to have it, and those who do feel guilty for enjoying it!

Sex is God's idea and everything God made is good! I have a saying in my classes: If you don't like sex, don't get married (*this excludes illness that prevents intimacy*). It's not fair for your mate to face a life of celibacy if that's not what you both agreed to beforehand. Going weeks and months without connecting on a physical level is cruel. The lack of it leaves a marriage vulnerable to attack from outside, meaning the temptation of another. Intimacy causes a husband and wife to bond together not only physically but spiritually.

Here are some common reasons wives don't want sex with their husbands:

- When you leave bad you get bad when you get home. Lovemaking starts in the morning. Kind words and a kiss goodbye go a long way toward setting the mood for lovemaking later.

- Nothing is sexier than a man washing dishes or running the vacuum cleaner. A wife who gets help with the chores is more likely to make love later, if for no other reason than she is not as tired, because hubby actually helped around the house. Help with the kids, because it's frustrating for a working mom to come home and continue to work for hours while their spouse watches TV. Stay-at-home moms need a break from the kids and chores. Husband, pitch in and help out!

- According to Dr. Brenda Wade, when a husband doesn't help around the house, his wife usually views sex as just another chore, another thing she has to do for someone else!

- Many husbands don't make any conversation or physical advances except at bedtime when they want sex. Ugh, that's such a turnoff!

- Abuse (verbal, physical, or sexual) is a killer of intimacy. The man who does this to his wife apparently doesn't ever want to have sex again! Who wants to make love with someone who puts them down, calls them names, or is physically abusive? Get help!

- Guilt from having pre-marital sex with their husband
- Fear of getting pregnant—get reliable birth control if you're not ready for a family
- Financial stress
- Exhaustion and lack of sleep, especially common with small children in the household
- Bitterness
- Medications, some list "lack of libido" as a side effect

What do men want? (Research comes up with the same answer repeatedly)

- Sexual fulfillment
- Respect
- To be needed

Marriage is honorable in all, and the marriage bed is undefiled. Hebrews 13:4a

Sex is God's idea—enjoy it! Although the marriage bed is undefiled, it doesn't mean we are allowed to make sex a kinky, freaky, free-for-all. Defecating, urinating, or inflicting pain on a spouse should never take place in the Christian marriage bed, or any marriage bed for that matter. It's not a sin to buy your wife lingerie and stilettos. It is a sin to ask her to wear a dog collar and crawl around on the floor. Degrading your spouse is sin.

Not in the mood, ladies? Pray for your heart to burn with passion for your spouse. God cares about all of things that concern His people and low sex drive or lack of libido is important to Him if it is important to you. Pray for your heart to burn with passion for your spouse. He will answer this prayer. Visit your doctor to discuss the medications you are taking and their side effects. Also, ask about medications that increase libido if necessary. Be open and honest with your spouse and your physician so you can get help if this is a medical condition.

What about oral sex? We always get this question whenever we teach a marriage class. The Bible does not specifically mention oral sex as being sin and I am not of the opinion that there is a problem with it as foreplay. However, it should never replace physical intercourse. It is up to each individual couple to decide what role if any this act will take in their marriage bed. I do believe it is wrong to force any act on your spouse if it is not something they wish to do. The marriage bed is undefiled, but force or coercion is wrong if it offends your spouse.

What about anal sex? What does the word of God say on the matter? It mentions homosexuality as sin, and the act of anal sex does not meet God's command to multiply and be fruitful. It does not bring forth fruit, it is extremely unsanitary, and can cause serious bacterial infection in women such as Trichomoniosis, and in both sexes possibly AIDS.

The body is not meant for sexual immorality. 1 Corinthians 6:13
Lord forgive my hidden sins, may they not have rule over me. Then I will be blameless, and innocent of great transgression. Psalm 19: 12-14

Prayer: Heavenly Father, help me to lovingly share my body with spouse and forgive me for using my body for sexual immorality in the past and let me glorify You from this moment forward.

Unmet Needs

Mistake # 8: No respect for the needs of your spouse

Know what your spouse needs and meet those needs

I think we focus so much on our own needs that we forget to meet the needs of our spouse. The new buzz phrase of today's youth is, *"I'm gonna do me first"*, which means I'm going to make sure I'm taken care of first and above all else.

Taking your spouse on their dream trip to England or Hawaii and playing golf or shopping the entire time instead of spending time together is not meeting each other's needs. The idea is to compromise and do what you both want. The best marriages know compromise is a key to success. No one gets their own way all time it just isn't possible. Never assume a quiet spouse means an agreeing spouse. Read body language and watch attitudes. You may have a ticking time bomb on your hands.

I have heard more dismayed spouses say they came home one day and their spouse was just gone or packing to go. Almost always the left spouse is taken totally off guard, because they thought everything was fine and thought they had a happy marriage. Maybe you were happy, but it is obvious your spouse wasn't. No one just leaves. They always drop subtle hints—no lovemaking, not talking, and no quality time together are pretty good signs something is wrong. Be mindful of the needs of your spouse and try and meet them.

• Pray for each other daily

• Value each other's opinion

• Bless each other with your words

• Side with your spouse

• Maintain a united front when it comes to the children

• Share in financial decisions

• Admit when making a mistake and apologize

• Give yourself freely to each other sexually

• Create a peaceful home environment

Let nothing be done through strife or vainglory; but in lowliness of mind let each esteem others better than themselves. Philippians 2:3

Being Overextended

Mistake # 9: Too busy with career, church, etc.

Burning yourself out with church work won't help your marriage

Being overly busy is a major mistake of not only newlyweds, but also many couples married for years. The biggest threat to intimacy between a husband and wife is not spending quality time together. You grow apart when you don't spend time together.

When God's word admonishes us to *occupy until He comes*, He did not mean for us to occupy every minute of our available time. Christians in this fast-paced society have made the wrong assumption that running themselves ragged equals righteousness. We have quickly become a people that have to fill every minute of our free time. We feel guilty about taking a moment to spend with our family. There's a scripture in the Old Testament that talks about a newlywed husband taking a year off to make his wife happy.

When a man is newly married, he shall not go out with the army or be charged with any business; he shall be free at home one year and shall cheer his wife whom he has taken. Deuteronomy 24:5

Somehow we took on the belief that a busy Christian is a more desirable Christian. Many churches unfortunately seek out willing workers who will say yes to everything. Sadly still, they say yes to everything. They serve on every committee, get burned out, and then leave the church altogether. Not taking on too much will prevent that from happening to you. When surveyed, the adult children of Charismatic parents who walked away from God as adults stated the number one reason was they resented church, because their parents were always there and not at home spending time with them. Don't make your spouse or children compete with the church for your attention.

Many unsaved spouses have this very complaint. They don't like coming home to an empty house because you've put more time in your ministry than your marriage. Now you're so overextended that you don't have the energy to enjoy your spouse

The statistic that says "20% of the people handle 80% of the workload" is an all too familiar indictment concerning church involvement. My word to the 20%—stop it! You are not solving the problem, you are unwittingly adding to it. Give someone else a chance to handle the various necessary functions of the church or ministry. Take some time with your spouse! Remember: it's God first, family second; not God first, church second, job third, family somewhere at the bottom.

How to balance marriage and ministry

1. Just say no!

2. Set reasonable limits to your involvement in everything

3. Learn to read your family meter. Are your children and spouse complaining about the lack of family time?

4. Ask God what He might have you participate in. His answer may surprise you!

5. The Bible says to listen diligently to the voice of the Lord. If any man lacks wisdom let him ask of the Lord

6. Pray before you become involved in any ministry

7. Know when to take break from ministry

8. Be obedient! It is better than sacrificing your family

9. Wait! Waiting on God doesn't mean you'll never get your chance

10. When God tells you to move in ministry, He'll make way for your gift

Family should not be sacrificed for ministry. Does your family know they are important to you, more important than ministry? The Bible says to be faithful in what He has already given you. He has given you a family, so be faithful in that first. No one will admire your ministry if your marriage is in shambles and your children are unsaved. Those who suffer burnout are usually overburdened and doing work God has not called them to do. God does not want you to win the world for Him and loose your own family in the process.

Remember these key things

• If you are under stress it will affect the whole family

• Time is the greatest gift you can give your spouse and children besides Jesus

• God gives strength to the faint and weary (Isaiah 40:29)

• Those who wait upon the Lord shall renew their strength (Isaiah 40:30)

• God's yoke is easy and His burden is light (Matthew 11:30)

• The Bible says it's the little foxes that spoil the vines, not the big things. Don't keep adding little things to your work load.

How do you know your ministry is threat to your marriage?

- Do you feel stretched, stressed, anxious, fatigued?
- Do you constantly worry about your children and the state of your marriage?
- Are you overly concerned with what people will think of you if you miss a service, meeting, or a Sunday school class?
- Do you feel if you don't attend Bible school classes someone will get ahead of you or take the spot you've mapped out or claimed for yourself?
- Do your children complain and whine about going to church as you drag them out the door again?

One of the biggest reasons pastors' kids don't go to church as adults is the complaint that all they did growing up was go to church! Do they feel church work is more important than the family? Do they see church as a competition for your time and attention? Some adult children of Christians feel their parents ministered more to others and neglected their needs. One of the biggest reasons unsaved spouses don't go to church is the same resentment. When asked, many say all their spouse does is go to church, preach at them, and they never spend time or goes anywhere together.

No one can do it all, and it is futile to try. It can be detrimental to your mental, emotional, and physical well-being. If you say you'll devote more time to your marriage and kids when this project is over, you'd better hope you still have them when you're through.

If you are too tired to nurture a relationship as vital as your marriage, then you're too busy, period. There is no such thing as a maintenance-free marriage. You keep ignoring it and you'll have disastrous results. If your marriage is in trouble, suffering burnout, or has just fizzled out, you will be relieved to know God has some answers for you.

Financial Failures and Fiascoes

Mistake # 10: Underestimating the strain of financial pressure on marriage

It's said, when poverty comes, love flies out the window

Don't start your marriage off trying to keep up with the Joneses. Overspending can seriously hurt your marriage. Don't get to the point where you dread opening the mail or answering the phone.

The leading cause for divorce is not infidelity, its financial stress. Why we Americans work to live so far above our means is still a mystery. Trace back to the invention of the credit card and instant gratification and you've got the answer. American's are filing bankruptcy in record numbers and Credit Counseling is a booming business.

Most couples start their marriages in debt with a big, elaborate wedding ceremony they can't afford and no one will remember except them. Years ago, most women married right after high school and while still living with mom and dad who foot the bill, set reasonable limits, and kept tight control on the spending. However, the average bride is over twenty-five years old and living on her own, so she and the groom find themselves splitting the cost. This on top of the huge college loans they brought into the marriage makes the financial stress greater.

Don't start off so far in debt that you feel you need to work more than one job or constant overtime to not even break even. Then you've got the issue of increased interoffice affairs, because people are spending more time with co-workers than spouses! Set attainable goals like saving for a house, vacation, furniture, new car, and that life time expense—children! Our parents' generation had layaway instead of credit cards. They had to make payments on items they couldn't afford to purchase immediately, but they didn't have to avoid opening mail or answering the phone!

Be a good and wise steward of what God has given you. Try to pay a little above the minimum payment on credit cards, cook meals at home several nights a week and make eating out a treat not the norm. The average specialty coffee drinker spends over $200 a month just on gourmet coffee. Imagine what you're spending on dinners and lunches out. Plan and stick to a budget. Contact creditors and make arrangements to pay what you can afford. Dodging creditors only hurts you. Contact a reputable credit counseling service that's been approved by the Better Business Bureau.

All Christians should be tithing. If you don't you are not only robbing God, you are cheating yourself. You will always be short each month if you don't tithe. It tells God you don't trust Him to handle your money and meet your needs. If you say you tithe but are still in debt, think about how long it took you to get in debt. Unless you had temporary amnesia and went on a one-day spending binge, you did not get into trouble overnight. You have had a long history of over spending, so don't expect to get out overnight. If you need help, attend a shopaholic's support group or see a financial counselor. Ask God to help you and give you strategies to get out of debt.

Here are a few tips:

- Negotiate a payment schedule with your creditors

- Only use credit cards for an emergencies

- Cut up the ones you don't need

- Close the accounts of the ones you aren't using

- Attempt to pay off the accounts with the lowest balances first

- Once one bill is paid use that money toward another account. Keep this pattern going and slowly but surely you will get out of debt.

- Once you are in a position to, put some money in savings at a different bank so you won't just transfer the money to your checking account

Find ways to save every day

- Use a discounted market, where you have to use your own shopping bags

- Delete some of those cable channels

- Buy a previously owned car instead of a new car

- If you have an old car, find a trustworthy, reliable mechanic

- Don't try to compete with older, more established couples. They don't have small children and have a lot more disposable income

- Don't have children until you get your finances under control

- Don't eat out every day. Brown bag your lunch.

- Budget and plan meals
- Work together as a family to make and keep a budget
- Seek God in everything; He has the answer to everything

About the author

Risa Pleasant and her husband Mark have been married for twenty-seven years. They are graduates of Total Word Bible Institute in Inglewood, California. Both are ordained ministers and have also been church planters and missionaries. They have taught newlywed and engaged couples' classes for the past eleven years as well as oversee Union Keepers, a marriage ministry at Bethel Temple in Hampton, Virginia. They have a twenty-five year old daughter and a twenty-two year old son. You can reach them by email at rkpleasant@juno.com

WORKBOOK

Commitment is the Key

Answer these questions or statements:

What am I prepared to do to stay married?

_____

_____

_____

Have I thought about life beyond my wedding day?

_____

Have we discussed having children, how many, and when? _____

_____

_____

What are my goals for marriage, a home, job security, schooling, rent, childcare, etc? _____

_____

Am I really committed to this marriage, even when things aren't perfect or go my way? _____

_____

Do I have trouble keeping a promise or honoring my word? _____

If so, am I willing to work on changing that behavior?

_____

Old Things are Passed Away

Take a moment to reflect on your family history.

What areas of weakness do I need to work on, as well as commit to prayer? _____

_____

_____

_____

Is divorce an option? Do I have a "plan B" in case this doesn't work? _____ _____

If the answer is yes or maybe, you are not ready for marriage.

These are family patterns that I don't want to carry into my new marriage. *Use this as a prayer list for your marriage.*

_____

_____

Which marriages do I admire? Why? _____

_____

_____

Find one of these couples and ask them to mentor you. Be accountable to them for advice and friendship.

Determination plays a major role in having a successful marriage. Am I determined to have a successful marriage? _____

_____

Compensation for My Pain and Suffering

Am I carrying any emotional baggage? What? _____

_____

What am I doing to alleviate any emotional baggage that could affect my marriage? _____

_____

_____

Am I aware there is Christian counseling available to me? (*Always select a licensed therapist or counselor*)

_____

_____

Do I realize it is not fair to make my spouse pay for the hurt and pain caused by others? _____

_____

Am I aware that emotional well-being is as important as physical well-being? _____

_____

Does mental illness or depression run in my family?

_____

Am I hiding a secret that can destroy my marriage?

_____

What areas do I plan to work on to make myself a more emotionally mature and committed person?

_____

_____

Fair Fighting

Am I aware that confrontation is a normal part of life?

_____

Do I have a win-at-all-cost personality? _____

Am I aware that using this technique in an argument can destroy my chances of a long-term marriage?

_____

Do I swear or become aggressive when in an argument? _____ _____

Do I take losing badly, even if the other person may be right? _____

Do I have anger management issues and loose control easily?_____

If you do, please seek professional help.

Am I afraid of confrontation and avoid it at any cost?

_____

Not speaking up for yourself is unhealthy. Let your spouse know you are having trouble verbalizing your feelings. Practice verbalizing your feelings to someone you trust.

I agree to no name-calling or physical violence. I will fight fairly with my spouse. _____

Based on my upbringing, is my attitude about marriage negative or positive? _____

What is my birth order? _____

Sometimes when an older child marries a younger child, they can revert to those roles inside the marriage. Be sure to start off on equal footing.

Do I get along well with my siblings? _____

If not, why? _____

If not, have I tried to repair the rift? _____

How long have my parents been married? _____

Do my parents model the example of a good marriage?
_____

If my parents are divorced, do I feel I've learned from their mistakes? _____

If not, what can I do to change that opinion and make my marriage work?

_____

_____

_____

_____

_____

Forgiveness

Do I realize that forgiveness and a successful marriage go hand-in-hand?_____

I will commit to walking in forgiveness on a daily basis.

_____

When I say I have forgiven my spouse, do I mean it?

_____

I will stay in the present when arguing and not bring up the past _____   _____

I realize that by forgiving my spouse means I will not seek revenge? _____

I commit to resolving conflict quickly and not holding a grudge _____

I'm aware that if I choose not to verbalize my true feelings; I open the door to possibly being misunderstood by my spouse? _____

_____

What can I do to keep conflict to a minimum and apply forgiveness to my daily life? _____

_____

My Work Here is Finished

I plan to continue dating after marriage _____

Our budget allows us to date weekly, bi-weekly or monthly? _____

How do I plan to save for dates? _____

Will we take turns planning dates? _____

Suggestions for no-cost dates _____

_____

_____

Suggestions for dates under $10 _____

_____

_____

Suggestions for dates under $25 _____

_____

Suggestions for dates $50 or more _____

_____

_____

Sex is Important

I know sex is God's idea and intended for pleasure

_____

I am aware that lovemaking is a normal and healthy part of married life _____

_____

I am prepared to get help for any sexual hang ups I might have _____

I've identified my emotional baggage and worked through it _____

Prior to marriage, we discussed birth control and when to start a family _____

_____

Prior to marriage, we discussed reliable birth control with a physician if we are not ready for children

_____

We will not feel pressured into having a child before we are ready and feel comfortable and secure in the marriage_____

I believe I can have a healthy sex life without guilt

_____

Unmet Needs

My marital needs and expectations are _____

_____

_____

_____

I have asked my spouse what their marital needs and expectations are _____

_____

I commit to pray for my spouse daily_____

I value and respect my spouse's opinion _____

My family respects my spouse and understands that I expect this from them?_____

_____

I plan to support and to encourage my spouse by

_____

_____

_____

_____

_____

Being Over-extended

We've discussed what ministry we will participate in

_____

I realize that I don't need to be in every ministry

_____

I can commit to a ministry for a year or two. I know it doesn't have to be a lifetime commitment and I can change or try something new _____

We've agreed to not become overextended in our personal life and church duties _____

We've discussed overtime on the job_____

We will spend quality time together weekly _____

Our ideas for weekly quality time are _____

_____

_____

Financial Failures

Who should pay the bills _____

Who should manage the budget _____

We've discussed whether the wife should work

_____

We've discussed daycare options _____

What things do we really need? _____

_____

_____

What are our wants? _____

_____

_____

_____

We will save for those things by_____

_____

_____

We've set financial goals for a home or car by _____

_____

_____

_____

Made in the USA
Middletown, DE
31 October 2015